Old Glasgow Shops

by

Rudolph Kenna

Strathclyde
ARCHIVIST

First published in 1996 by
Strathclyde Regional Archives
Mitchell Library
North Street
Glasgow G3 7DN

ISBN 0 9517010 1 0

A CIP catalogue record for this book is available from the British Library.

Typeset and printed by
The Printing Works,
197 Pollokshaws Road, Glasgow G41 1TL
Telephone 0141-249 4614/26

Front Cover: Bow's emporium, High Street, c. 1900

Back Cover: Trongate, looking west, c. 1900. Moore, Taggart & Company's elegant Tontine
House (formerly the Tontine Hotel) and Daly & Company's mock baronial Tron House
(middle background) were among the prominent emporia in this famous shopping centre.

Introduction

Shops are of great antiquity, but it was not until the 19th century that they took on a recognisably modern shape. In 17th century Glasgow, as in Pompeii and Herculaneum, shops were essentially booths with wooden shutters. Permanent shops were scarce until the 18th century. In previous centuries most people purchased goods and services in the market place. In Glasgow wooden stalls were set up on market days in the vicinity of the 'mercat cross', which stood where the principal streets of the compact little town converged. In 1749 William Colquhoun opened Glasgow's first shoe shop, and the following year Andrew Lochart opened a drapery shop in the Saltmarket.

In bygone days, shop signs were essential, since only a small minority could read. The glover hung out an outsize glove, the grocer a sugar loaf, the locksmith a key, and the cordwainer (shoemaker) a boot. The hairdresser's red-and-white striped pole and the pawnbroker's three brass balls survive to remind us of the practice. In the early 1800s the Banditti Club, a disagreeable association of affluent young ruffians, caused a great deal of inconvenience in Glasgow by switching shop signs around.

The elegant bow-fronted shops of the late-18th century are familiar from engravings of the period. The typical Georgian shopkeeper was a retail tradesman, living on or near his premises. Each shopkeeper had special skills: grocers had to blend, grind, weigh and package much of their stock, and butchers were frequently their own slaughtermen. In those days the *modus operandi* of shopping was very different from that of today. Stock was stored in cupboards and boxes; many articles had to be made to order from designs in pattern books, and it was customary to haggle over prices. Cash sales at fixed prices would have struck the average trader as a very eccentric way of doing business, and he would have marvelled at the docility of the modern shopper.

Shopkeepers supplying the 'carriage trade' were extremely snobbish, treating the gentry with nauseating obsequiousness. The well-to-do expected and received credit as a matter of course. Much would change in the 19th century; a new breed of shopkeepers duly abandoned time-honoured practices in favour of cash sales, a quick turnover and smaller profit margins. Their motto was 'small profits and quick returns', and since they knew that people of modest means were cost-conscious, they attached price tickets to their wares.

These entrepreneurs pioneered the art of advertising, and at night their shop fronts were brilliantly illuminated by lamps on hanging brackets—a crowd-pulling feature in an era of rudimentary street lighting. Grocer James Hamilton installed gas lighting in his Trongate shop as early as 1818. It was the first such illumination in Glasgow.

By 1819 Glasgow's shops were well-established and diverse, but street traders and hawkers still catered for a large section of the population. The main shopping centres were High Street, Gallowgate, Saltmarket, Trongate, Bridgegate, Glassford Street, Hutcheson Street and Candleriggs. There were 259 shops in the Gallowgate and 230 in the Trongate. In the course of the 19th century, fashionable shopkeepers gradually moved west, away from the congested and insanitary wynds and closes of the old town.

Robertson Stewart and John McDonald pioneered Buchanan Street as a commercial centre, opening their new wholesale drapery warehouse in a rented tenement there in 1826. The Argyll Arcade, designed in 1827 by John Baird, was the earliest shopping arcade in Scotland. Built by John Reid Robertson, an entrepreneur who had been favourably impressed by the famous *passages* of Paris, it linked Argyle Street with Buchanan Street and helped to transform both streets into busy retail shopping centres. The Argyll Arcade was an attractive example of the new shopping fad, with a glazed roof of timber and 'hammerbeam' cast iron and elegantly proportioned shop fronts of timber and glass. Originally the Arcade contained a variety of shops, but it now functions as Glasgow's jewellery centre.

By 1837, Buchanan Street had become Glasgow's most exclusive shopping promenade, where luxuries such as ladies' London and Paris prints and gentlemen's rosewood dressing-cases were offered for sale. Messrs Kemp, Pringle and Lawson, of 47 Buchanan Street, stocked ' . . . a splendid choice of French and British long shawls or plaids in all the most fashionable colours, at prices from fifty shillings to twenty pounds' and also offered 'a superb choice of square shawls of French, Norwich, Edinburgh and Paisley manufacture at prices very much reduced.'

In the Victorian era Glasgow became a major distributing centre. Wholesalers began to amass large and varied stocks which they then proceeded to sell to retailers throughout the country. The wholesale warehouses of Victorian Glasgow, clad in the borrowed finery of Venetian *palazzi,* rivalled those of Manchester; many have since been converted into luxury flats. Commercial travellers such as Neil Munro's immortal Jimmy Swan were the arbiters of fashion in the small towns of Scotland. In the early 1890s, Messrs Stewart and McDonald exported their drapery and fabrics to all parts of the globe and no fewer than seventy travellers represented the firm at home and abroad.

The department store came into its own during Queen Victoria's reign, when consumer goods began to pour from the factories and workshops in astonishing variety. John Anderson pioneered the practice of selling many different kinds of articles under one roof. Anderson progressed from a drapery shop in Clyde Terrace to a Jamaica Street store equipped with a 'museum and waxworks'. He then moved to Argyle Street, where Anderson's Royal Polytechnic, known to generations of Glaswegians as 'the Poly', was the principal landmark until replaced in the 1930s by Lewis's (now Debenham's) store.

Wylie and Lochhead's magnificent retail warehouse in Buchanan Street, a lofty cast-iron saloon surmounted by a glazed barrel vault, attracted enormous interest when it opened in the mid-1850s. In Wylie and Lochhead's and similar stores, for the first time, shoppers were encouraged to browse without incurring any obligation to make purchases.

House furnishings ostentatious enough to mirror the aspirations of the rising middle classes were displayed to advantage in the new department stores, Aladdin's caves crammed with carpets, pictures, gargantuan mahogany furniture, and hideous bric-a-brac—the tortured china and porcelain deemed indispensable to Victorian ideals of domesticity. During the same period, however, low-price retail shops were proliferating in the industrial districts to supply the modest needs of the new factory workers.

With liberally applied mouldings, elaborate brass gasoliers, a profusion of mirrors, and a plethora of ferns in china pots, the grand Victorian emporia offered newly affluent shoppers an ambience of luxury. But even quite small shops frequently boasted colourful tiled murals and richly embossed mirror advertisements for products such as Van Houten's Cocoa and Wright's Coal-Tar Soap.

In 1825, Robert Simpson opened a shawl warehouse at 154 Trongate. The business was transferred to Jamaica Street in 1851 and gradually extended until it occupied the entire Jamaica Street-Argyle Street corner. 'Simpson's Corner' became a famous Glasgow meeting place.

William Copland and John Lye opened their first shop in 1873 in Cowcaddens. The firm prospered, moving in 1878 to a grand new store, The Caledonian House, in Sauchiehall Street. By 1911 the attractions of Copland and Lye's included a ladies' lounge and an orchestra.

Sauchiehall Street is much the poorer for the loss of its three *grands magasins,* Copland and Lye's Caledonian House, Pettigrew and Stephens' Manchester House, and Tréron et Cie. In spite of its name, the latter lacked an authentic Gallic pedigree, for it was merely a branch of Walter Wilson's Colosseum. There is an apocryphal story to the effect than an irate female customer once demanded to see the mythical Mr Tréron. When told that he was unavailable, she then insisted on speaking to Mr Kye!

The handsome facade of Tréron's can still be seen, but The Caledonian House and The Manchester House were torn down in the 1970s to make way for a singularly unprepossessing shopping mall. A more recent loss was the enterprising Walter Wilson's Colosseum in Jamaica Street, a pioneering iron building, demolished in 1994. But elsewhere in the city, one can still see the frontages of several famous Victorian department stores. The turreted and gabled upper storeys of Daly and Company's mock-baronial fantasy, The Tron House, are still an eccentric feature of Trongate, while Ogg Brothers' distinctive warehouse at Paisley Road Toll has been converted into flats.

Christmas cheer came late to staunchly Presbyterian Scotland, but by the 1880s the leading Glasgow stores were vying to attract custom by means of lavish yuletide displays. As early as 1883, the Grand Toy Fair in Walter Wilson's Colosseum was illuminated with sixty Swan electric lamps and was described as 'the only toy department in Scotland to be lighted with electricity'. An estimated 26,800 people visited The Colosseum on Saturday, 20th December, 1890.

In 1890 Pettigrew and Stephens' Manchester House accommodated 'a real live Father Christmas', along with 'grand illuminated panoramic tableaux'. That same year, Copland and Lye's Caledonian House featured 'the enchanted castle of Santa Claus'. Up-to-date toys on display in Copland and Lye's 1905 Christmas Bazaar included wireless telegraphy apparatus, clockwork airships and submarines, and typewriters. Model shops, like teddy bears, were an early unisex toy. At Christmas 1907, Copland and Lye offered 'a great variety of toy shops', the most lavish of which cost several pounds.

By 1883 the big stores were already holding January sales—in The Caledonian House, ladies' flannel drawers were marked down from 4s to 2s 11d. Then as now, there were unrepeatable special offers. The Albani corset was 'shaped and cut upon hygienic principles', and every purchaser received, entirely free, 'a 4s piece of high-class music by eminent composers'. By 1893 Glasgow had succumbed to the football craze—W. G. Bell of Argyle Street were selling goalkeeper's gloves, leather shinguards, and 'football knickers' at 11s per pair. With thousands participating in football, cycling and 'pedestrianism' (jogging), grocers did a roaring trade in Bovril, glowingly described as 'the best muscle-forming drink for athletes'. For those too feeble to participate in the vogue for strenuous sports, Glasgow chemists dispensed 'Pearson's pink pills for pale people', manufactured in Oswald Street by George Pearson.

By the 1900s Argyle Street and Jamaica Street had become major shopping centres, much frequented by the working classes, but the most up-market shops were located in Buchanan Street, Gordon Street and Sauchiehall Street, as well as in the Argyll Arcade. In the aftermath of the International Exhibition of 1901, a Russian shop became one of the attractions of Sauchiehall Street, and the gilded youth of Edwardian Glasgow had a unique opportunity to dress *à la russe* and sample Caucasian mineral waters, Livadian white ports and Crimean cognac.

Sauchiehall Street and Buchanan Street retained their exclusive shopping character into the 1930s. In 1933 the official *City Guide* observed: 'Within the gorgeous and impressive salons of Sauchiehall Street and Buchanan Street, the latest creations of the Rue de la Paix are to be seen, objets d'art from every corner of the globe are there for the collector to acquire, and when from a surfeit of luxury the shopper desires a few well earned moments of rest, the numerous cafes, lounges and tearooms offer their welcome invitation.'

In the 1890s it was not unusual to find shop assistants working 90 hours a week. End of season sackings were particularly common in the drapery trade. The ease with which shop assistants could be hired and fired kept them in a state of servility and kept wages very low. Shop workers were dismissed virtually at a moment's notice, a practice which spelled misery for those who 'lived in' and found themselves not only out of a job, but homeless into the bargain. Margaret Bondfield, who began her early working life as a draper's assistant and later became Britain's first woman Cabinet Minister, helped to expose the iniquities of the 'living-in' system.

In 1908 there was a strike at Glasgow grocers J. and A. Fergusson, where the men worked 79 hours a week and the women 74, inclusive of mealtimes. There were no tea breaks, so some assistants were without sustenance from midday until 8.30 p.m. Many Edwardian shops closed around 9 p.m., but long after the shutters went up, the assistants would be at work scrubbing counters and stocking shelves. Under the provisions of the Shops Act of 1913, no assistant was to be employed for more than 65 hours in any week, exclusive of meal times.

In 1914 through an agreement between Galbraith's, the multiple grocers, and the Shop Assistants' Union, adult male employees secured a weekly wage of 36s, while females got 21s. In 1920 the staff of William Costigane's Bonanza and Granite House warehouses went on a one-day strike; some of the female assistants were receiving only 16s per week. In spite of legislation embodied in the various Shops Acts, progress was slow. In the Glasgow of the mid-1930s, a young male shop assistant's wages could be as low as 21s per week.

The first important innovation in shop design was glass, in the form of small brown or green rectangular panes. In the late-18th century, 'bottle glass' gradually gave way to 'white' or clear glass in moderately big squares, secured by wooden or metal glazing bars. The introduction of plate glass in the 1840s, and the repeal of the excise duty on glass in 1843, transformed the appearance of the streets of Glasgow and other large towns. By 1851, when the Crystal Palace was erected in London's Hyde Park, very large sheets of glass were being manufactured and iron-working technology was improving by leaps and bounds. Among the exciting new 'ferrovitreous' buildings inspired by the Crystal Palace were retail warehouses such as Gardner's (now Martin and Frost) in Jamaica Street, built in 1855-6.

Thanks to sheet glass and slim cast-iron colonnettes, Victorian shops had ample window space for display. Shop windows were frequently filled to capacity, every available inch of space being utilised. Such displays were highly popular in an era when few people had money to spare for amusements. Glasgow's own ebullient Thomas Lipton, doyen of Edwardian grocery magnates, was a pioneer of novel, crowd-pulling window displays, backed up by American-style advertising. Lipton opened his first shop in Stobcross Street in 1871; by 1898 he had over seventy branches in London alone. Multiple grocers such as Lipton catered increasingly for the working classes, who were enjoying a more varied diet, with access to cheap tea, eggs, bacon and cheese, and factory-processed tinned meats, sauces and jams.

In 1909 Gordon Selfridge brought advanced window dressing ideas over from America to his new store in London's Oxford Street. By the 1920s, many traders had abandoned traditional 'massed' display methods in favour of innovative 'open' window dressing. While heavily-dressed shops reminiscent of the Victorian era survived into the 1930s, they had become unfashionable. Shoppers were hurrying faster than ever before; some were sailing past in shiny new cars.

Only two 'shopfitters' are listed in the Glasgow Post Office Directory for 1876-77, while the Directory for 1912-13 lists no fewer than fifty-two. Not all the listed companies offered a full shopfitting service, however; some produced accessories such as advertising lamps, mirrors and sun blinds. Many Edwardian shops were representative of the 'Glasgow Style' of Art Nouveau. In the 1920s and 30's shop design was transformed by new ideas arriving from the Continent and the USA. Art Deco and Art Moderne flourished in the Glasgow of the inter-war period. Ciro Pearls Ltd in Buchanan Street (1926) survives in pristine condition, with bronze metal enrichments which reproduce Art Deco floral motifs associated with the 1925 Paris Exhibition of Decorative Arts.

Shop designers of the Twenties were influenced not only by the Paris Exhibition, but also by the Tutankhamun craze. The Thirties introduced another source of inspiration—pre-Columbian art. By the end of the period, designers were showing a preference for shiny, easy-to-clean surfaces such as vitrolite, faience, and chromed metal. Eye-catching Deco and Moderne fascia lettering was carried out in a wide range of materials. The new decorative vocabulary was applied to all kinds of shops, including multiples such as Burton's, 'the Fifty Shilling Tailors'.

While Victorian and Edwardian shop fronts were usually well-mannered, the new shops of the inter-war period frequently ignored the design and structure of older buildings, into which they were more often than not inserted. Deep fascias obliterated architectural mouldings and obscured first-floor windows; sub-Hollywood Moderne, not without intrinsic interest, was an incongruous addition to Glasgow's sooty, tenement-lined streets.

Luxury shops were sometimes designed by *avant garde* architects who managed to suggest quality and exclusiveness through the skilful use of fashionable materials such as glass bricks, anodized aluminium, and manganese bronze. Shop interiors became far less cluttered, and attractive decorative effects were obtained through the use of exotic wood veneers, peach mirrors and imaginative lighting fixtures. By the 1930s, display methods had achieved a high level of sophistication, with clever use of non-reflective glass, concealed lighting and such unusual features as oxidised metal backgrounds. Coloured neon was used with great flair in the 1930s. At night Deco and Moderne shops with neon-lit fascias were an advertising medium in their own right. By 1938, with the tentative revival of trade and industry, many Glaswegians were participating in a miniature consumer bonanza, soon to be curtailed by wartime rationing.

Shops continually renew themselves through changes in fashions, functions and owners. Late-Georgian shops with glazed bow windows were replaced by Victorian shops with lofty frontages of plate glass and cast-iron. These in turn were remodelled in the Art Nouveau style of the *fin de siècle*. The arrival of Deco and Moderne worked another, even more astonishing, transformation. In the Glasgow of today, many shops belong to giant chains or franchises and have little individuality; our streetscapes are all the poorer for such commonplace and ubiquitous house styles.

As late as the 1960s, Glasgow retained many shops that were culminatively representative of the changing fashions, foibles and technologies of the Victorian, Edwardian and inter-war eras. It is a pity that the opportunity was not taken to list a representative selection of these survivors before it was too late, and we have particular reason to regret the loss of 'Glasgow Style' shops of the early 1900s. But we can be thankful that the eye of the camera has helped to repair this omission by perpetuating memories of the formative years of shopping.

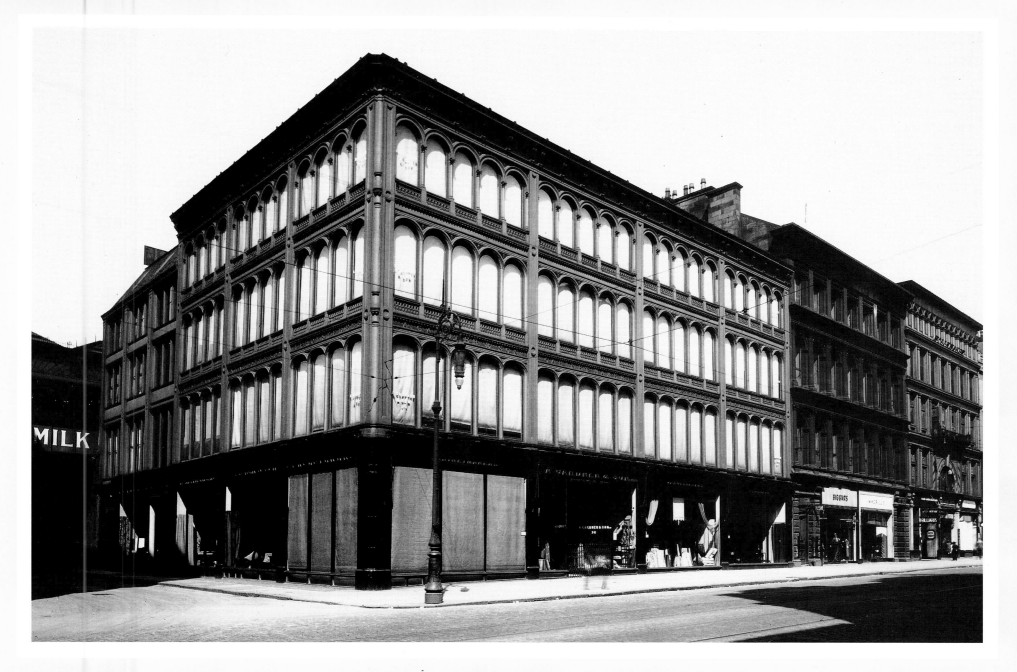

Archibald Gardner & Son's graceful warehouse in Jamaica Street celebrated mid-Victorian enthusiasm for plate glass and cast iron and was one of the first commercial buildings to copy the structural lessons of Paxton's Crystal Palace.

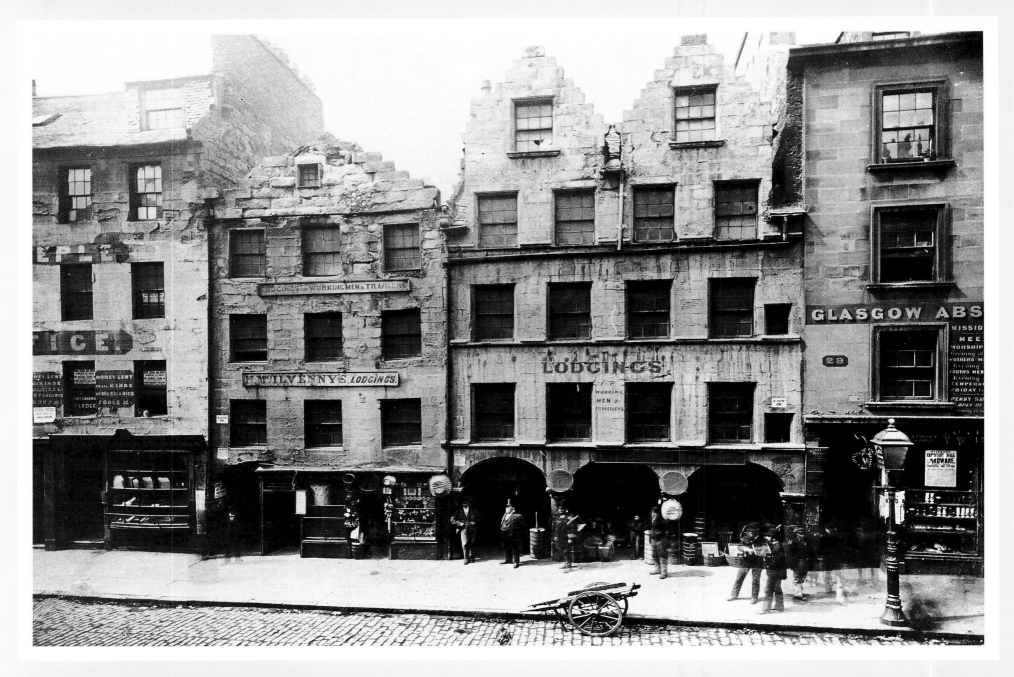

High Street c. 1868. The last of the arcaded shops, the famous 'piazzas' admired by Daniel Defoe
and other 18th century visitors to Glasgow, can be seen in the centre of the photograph.

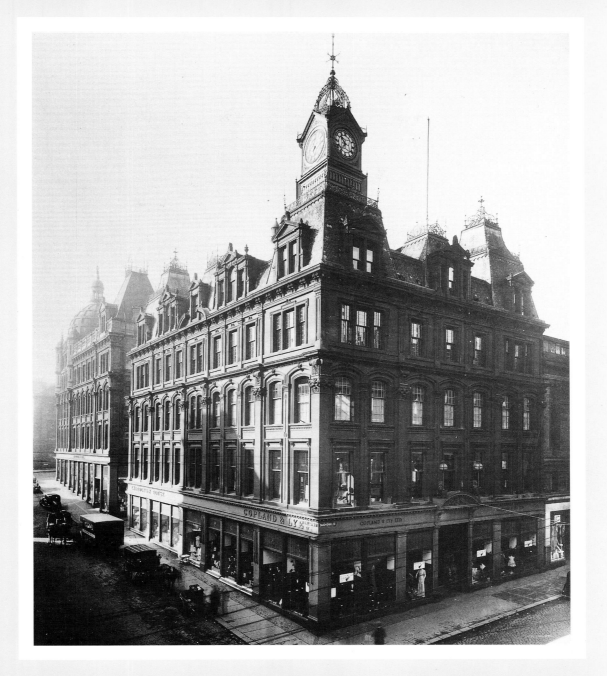

Copland & Lye's Caledonian House (1878) in Sauchiehall Street, as it appeared in the 1930s.

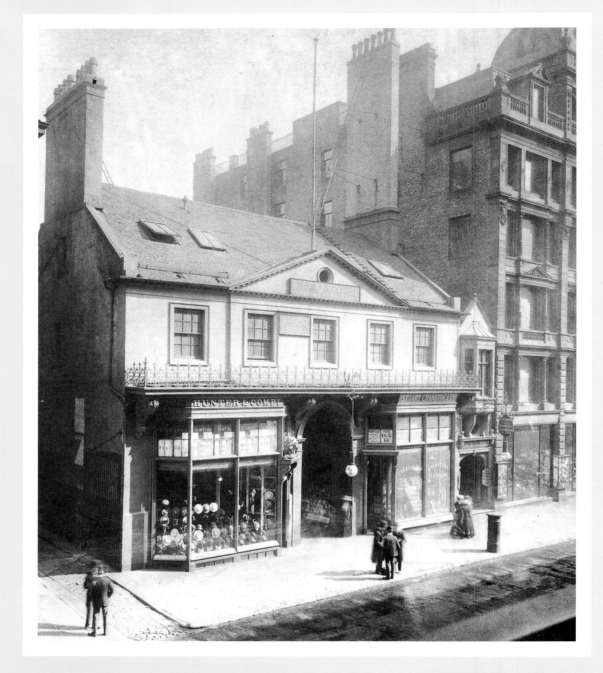

Buchanan Street, c. 1890, showing the original frontage to the Argyll Arcade. Stuart Cranston's tearooms, opened in 1889, are on the right of the entrance. In 1903 Cranston demolished the old frontage, replacing it with a tall Edwardian block.

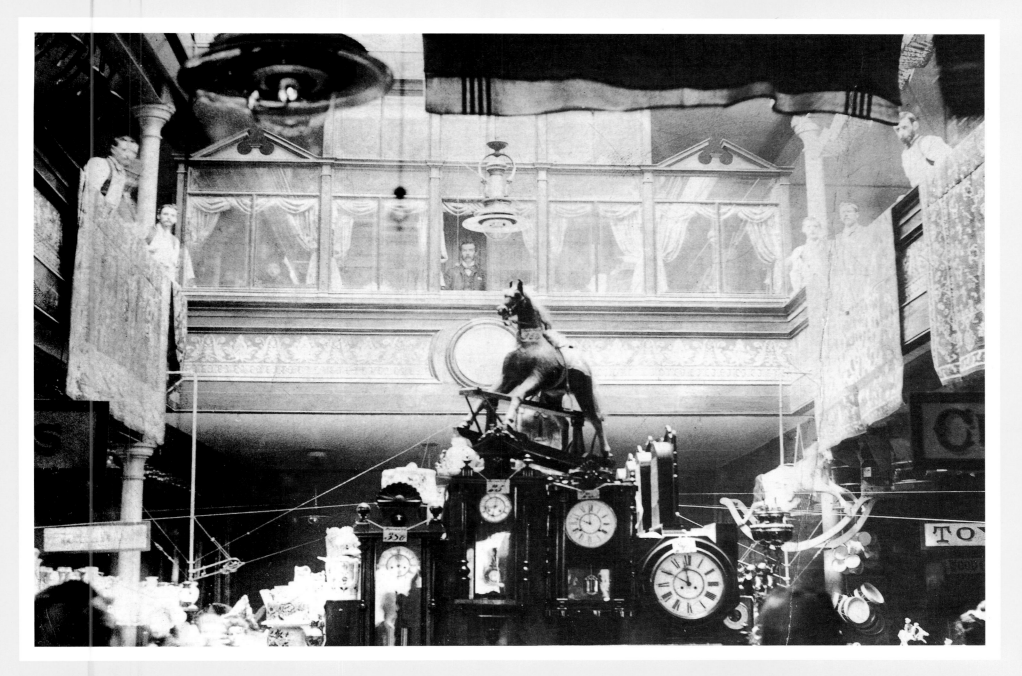

The interior of Bow's Emporium, 61-73 High Street, c. 1890. William Bow opened his first shop in the High Street in the early 1870s. His new Emporium was equipped with all the latest conveniences, including a cash railway.

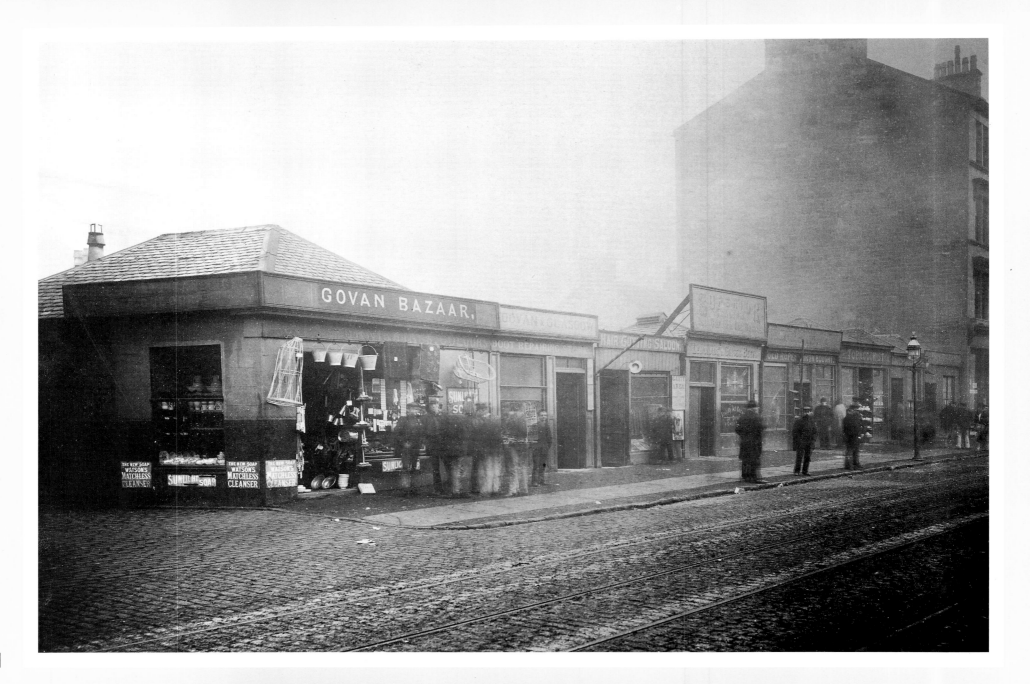

This row of shops in Renfrew Road, Govan, was photographed in 1890.

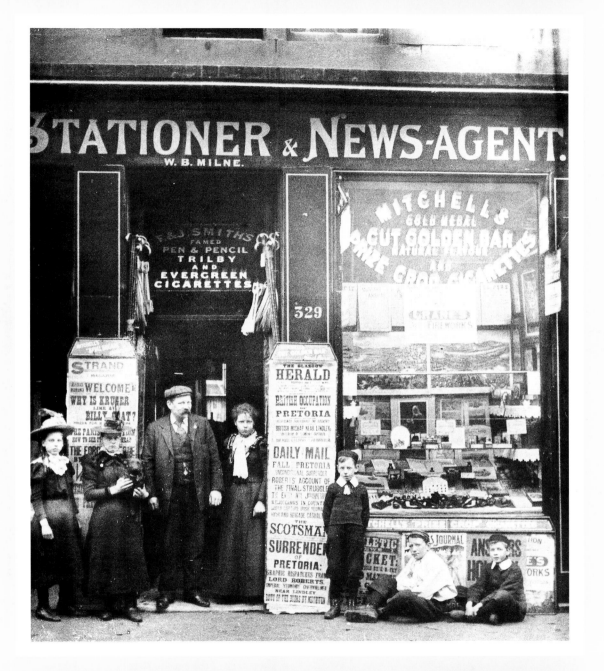

Newsagent's shop at 329 Springburn Road, 1900. Posters announce the surrender of Pretoria. Though celebratory fireworks are on sale, the South African War dragged on for another two years.

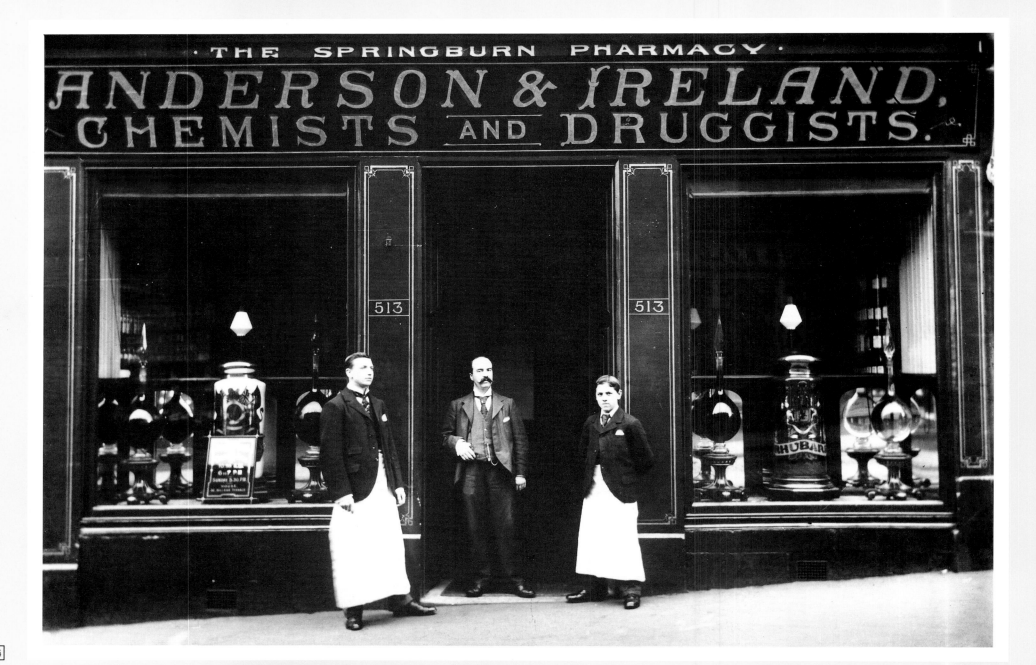

Chemist's shop at 513 Springburn Road, c. 1900. Note the ornate display bottles and jars.

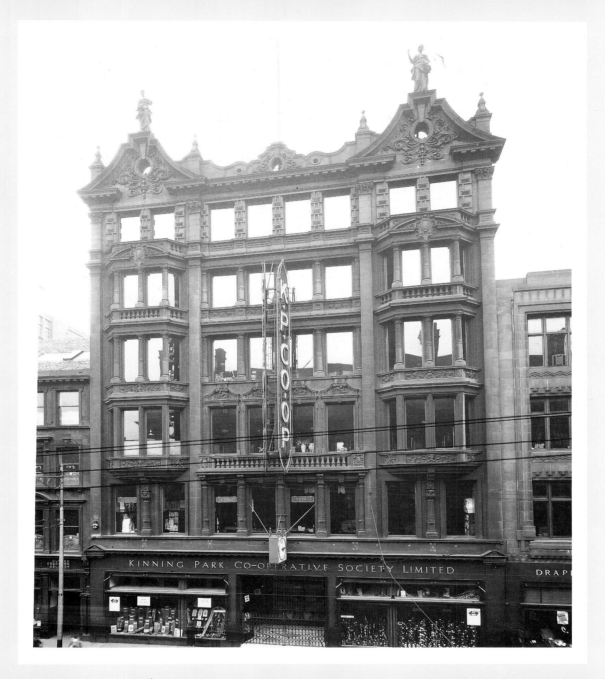

Kinning Park Co-op's highly ornate warehouse at 41-61 Bridge Street was designed by architects Bruce and Hay in 1902. The photograph was taken in 1939. By 1914, the SCWS was manufacturing everything from jam to dining room suites and had sold more than $2\frac{1}{2}$ million pairs of boots and shoes.

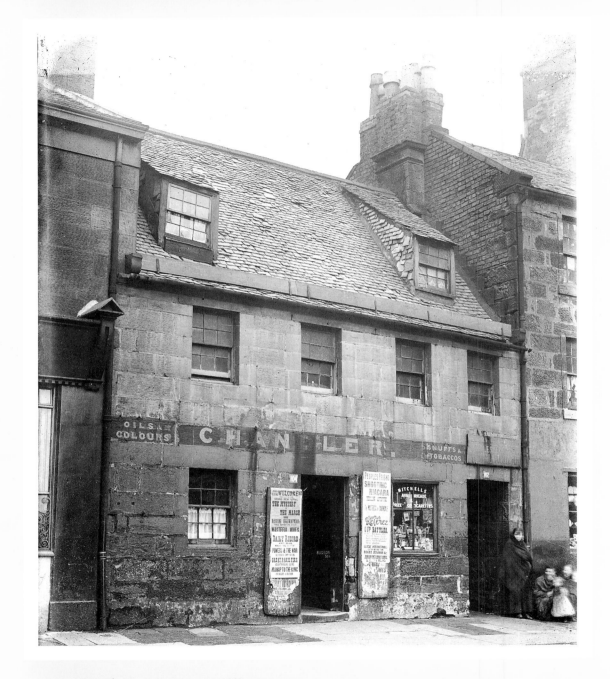

General store in Rottenrow, c. 1903.

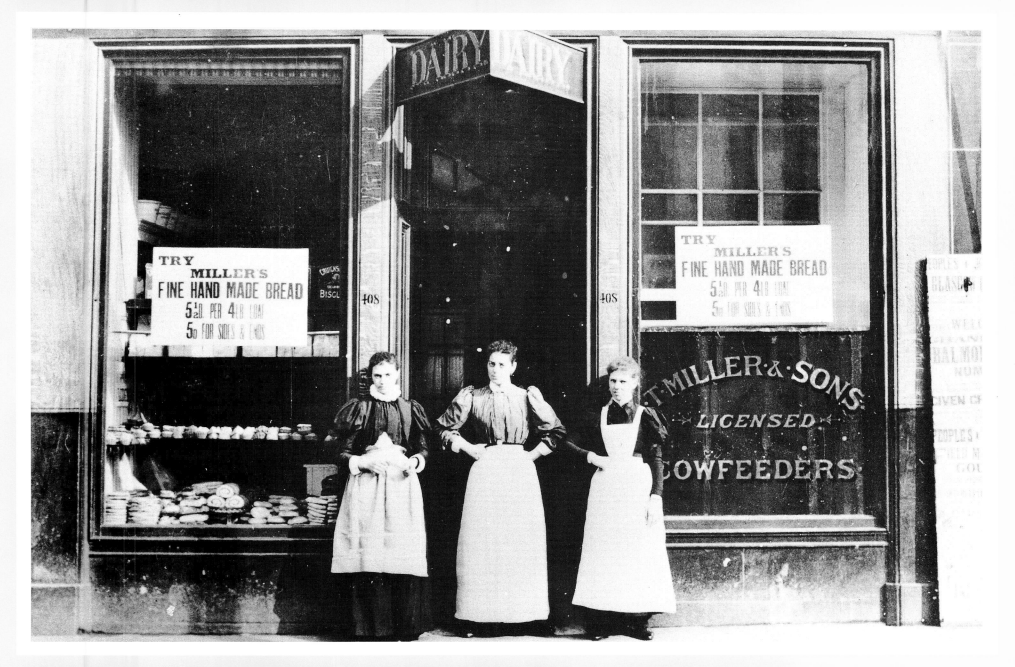

Employees outside Thomas Miller's dairy, 408 Springburn Road, c. 1903.

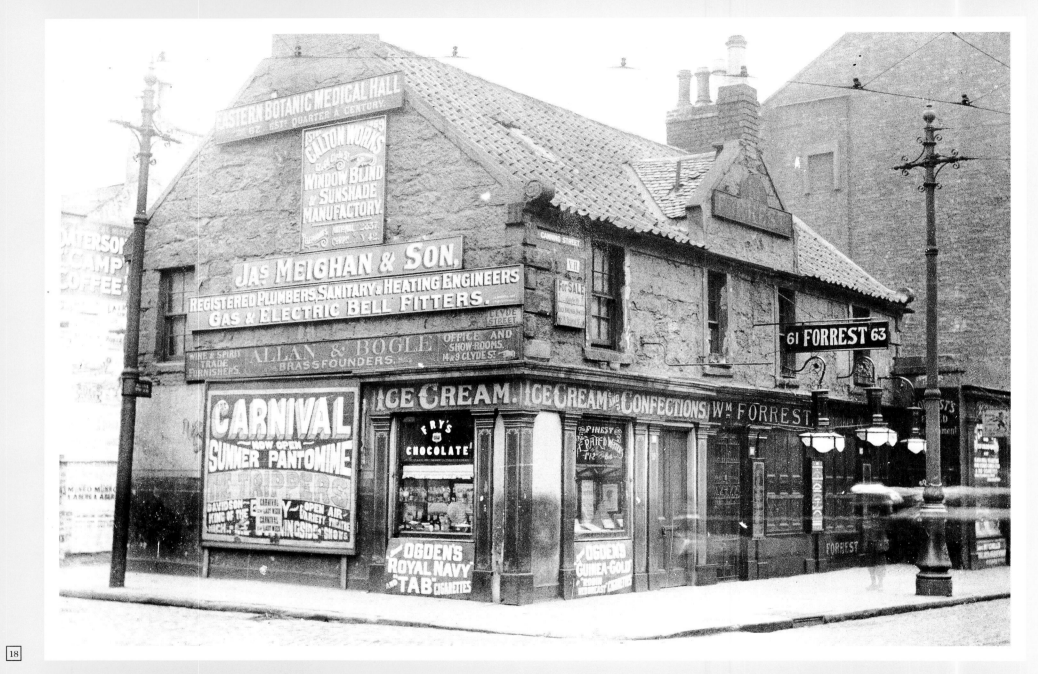

Small shop at the corner of Clyde Street and Canning Street (Calton), 1904.

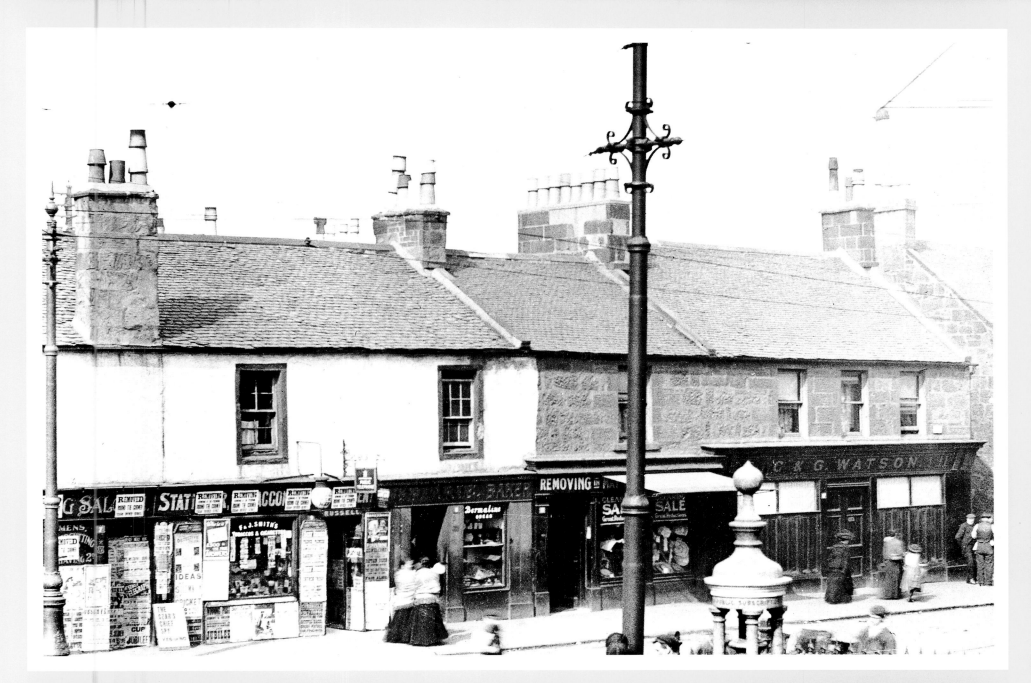

Shops in Westmuir Street, Parkhead, 1905.

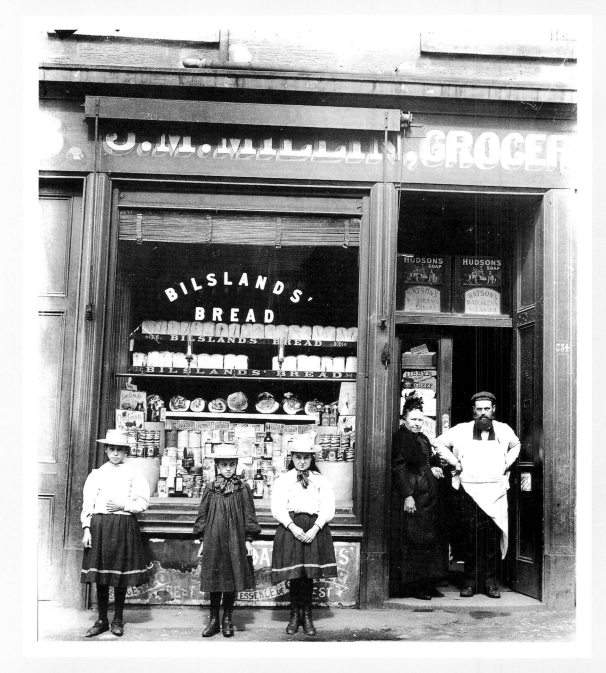

Grocer's shop at 734 Springburn Road, c. 1906. In summer straw 'boaters' were *de rigueur* for well-dressed schoolgirls.

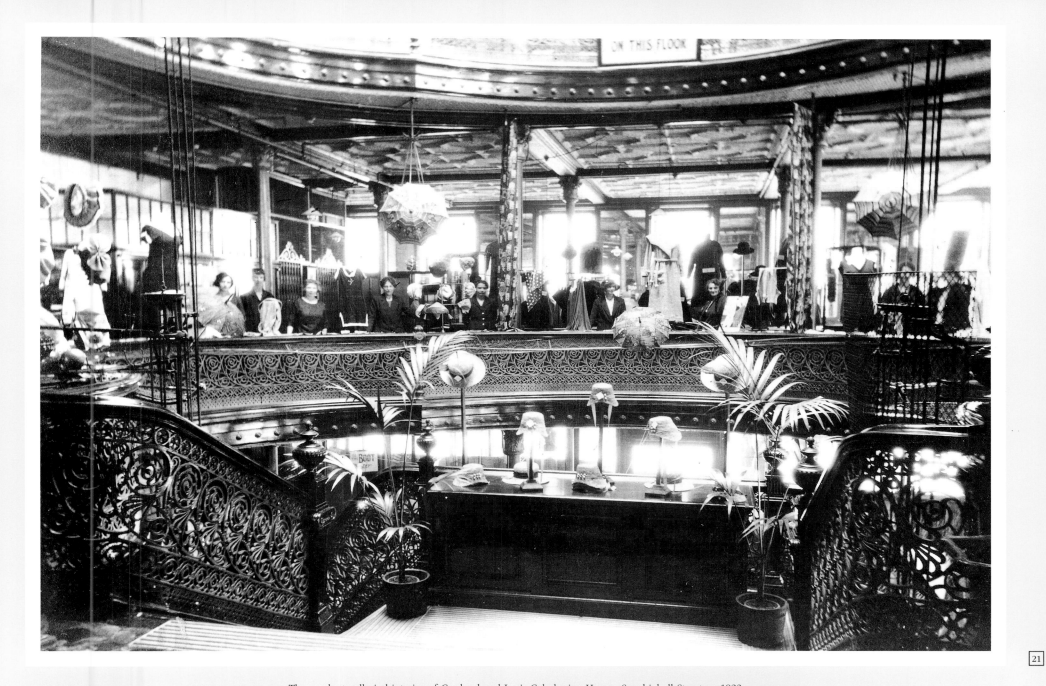

The opulent galleried interior of Copland and Lye's Caledonian House, Sauchiehall Street, c. 1922.

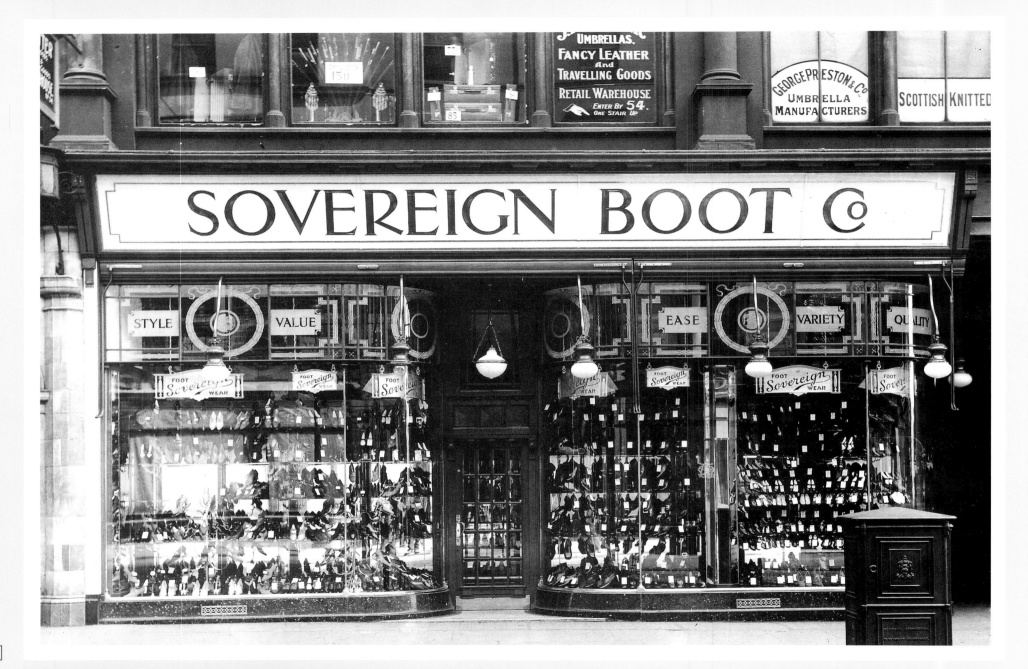

Boot and shoe shop in Union Street with traditional, heavily-dressed windows, 1923.

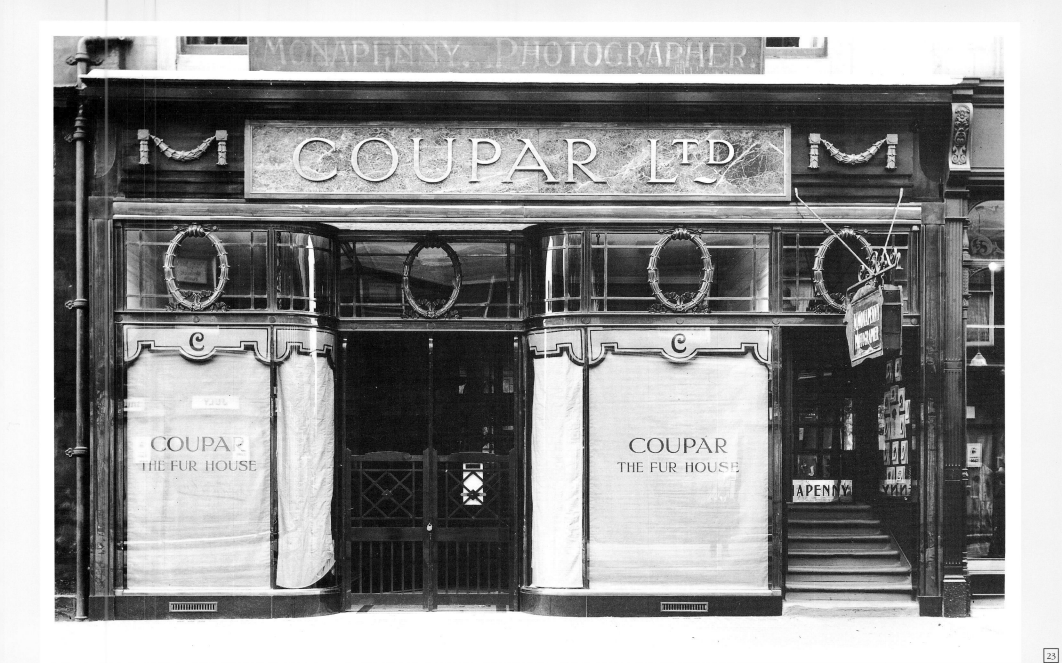

Prestige shopping 1920's style, embodied in the elegant premises of Coupar Ltd., 241 Sauchiehall Street. The photograph was taken in 1923.

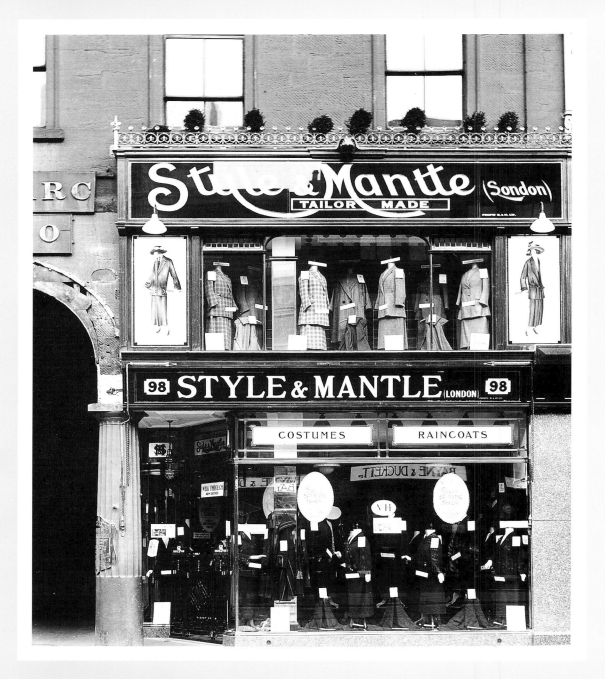

Costumiers at 98 Argyle Street, 1923. The first-floor window display was designed to catch the attention of passengers on the upper decks of trams.

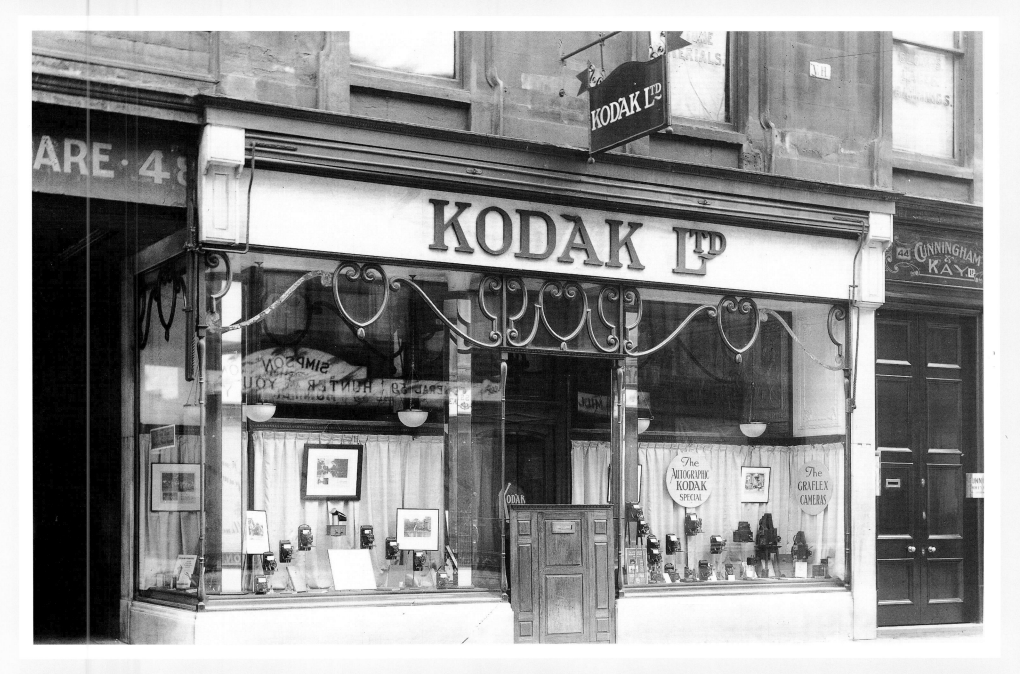

Kodak camera shop, 46 Buchanan Street, 1925. By the 1920s, inexpensive portable cameras and roll
films had brought photography within the reach of millions.

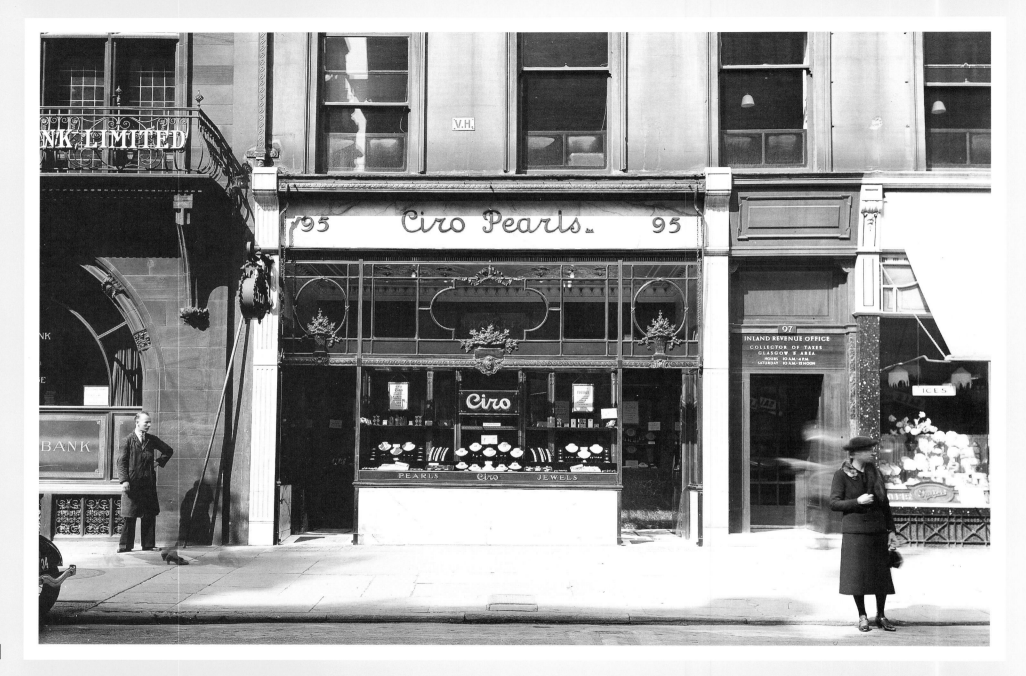

Ciro Pearls, 95 Buchanan Street, seen here in 1938, was designed in 1926 by George Boswell. The shop clearly shows the influence of the 1925 Paris Exhibition of Decorative Arts. At this period, bronze and marble were favourite materials for luxury shop fronts.

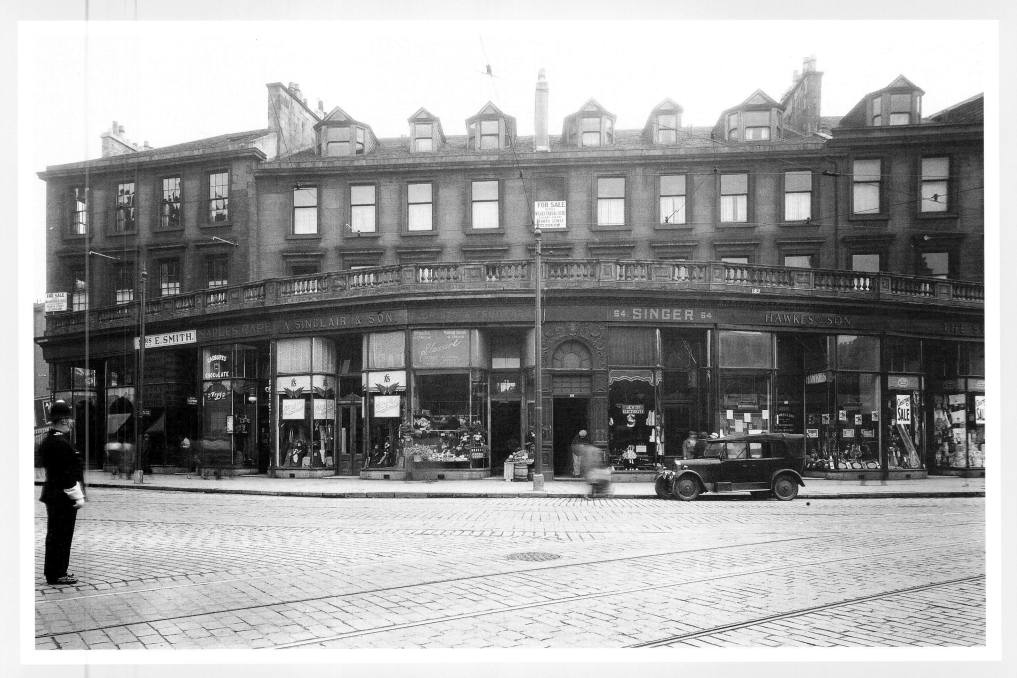

Well-mannered Edwardian shops in St. George's Road, 1930. The building was demolished to make way for the M8 motorway.

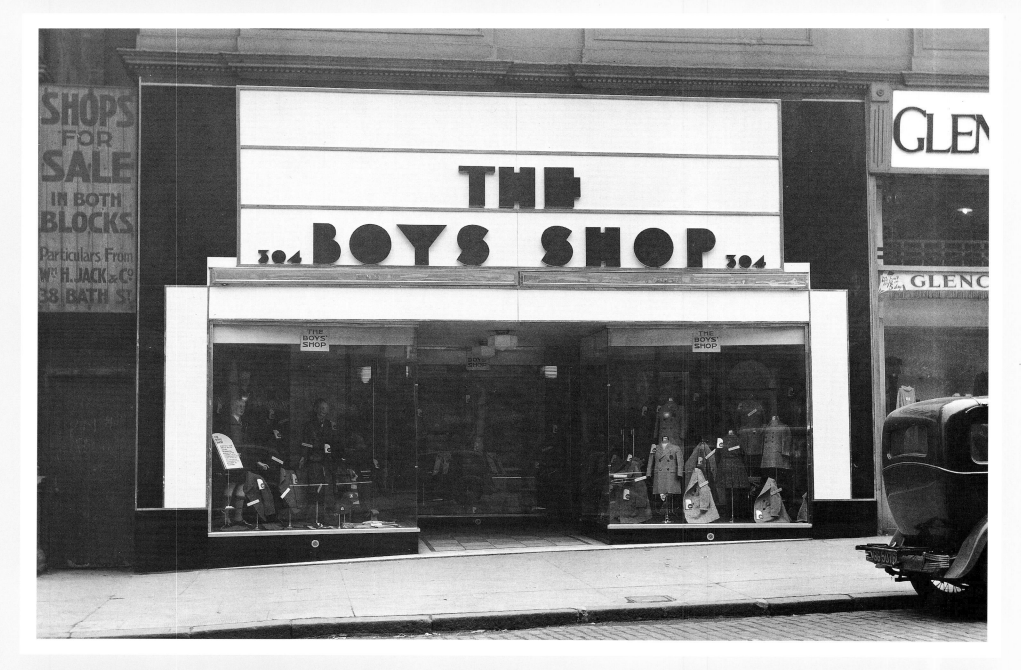

This shop at 304 Sauchiehall Street, photographed in 1931, features an eye-catching Art Moderne fascia.

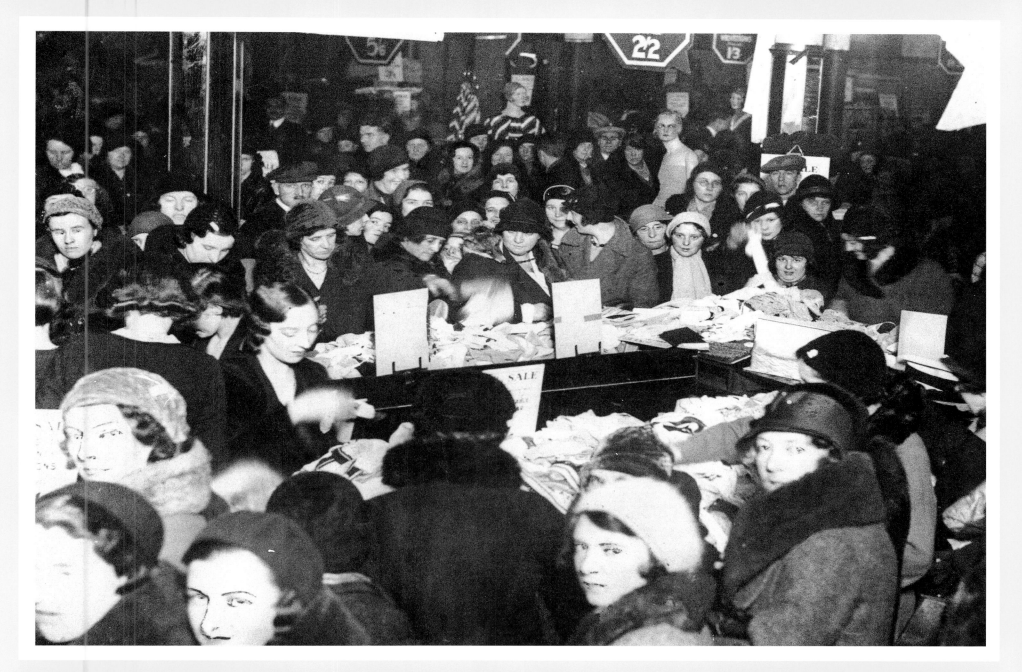

January Sale crowds in Anderson's Royal Polytechnic, Argyle Street, 1933.

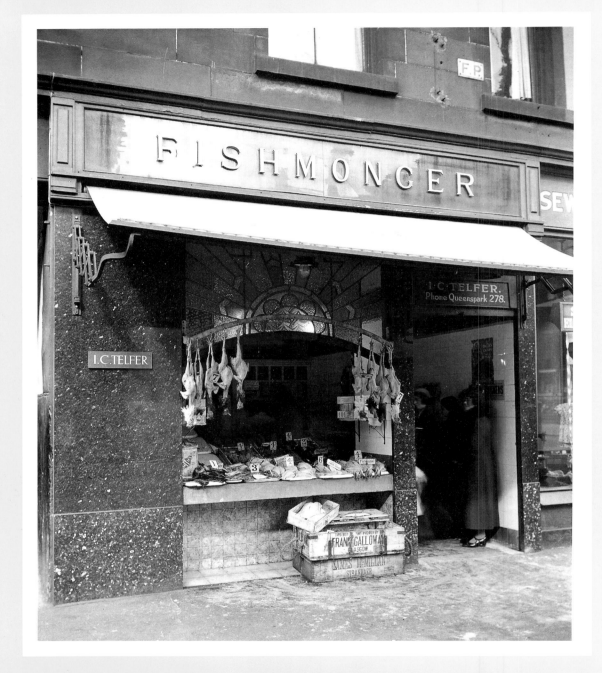

Fishmonger's shop at 490 Cathcart Road, c. 1934. The immensely popular Art Deco sunrise motif has been fashioned in leaded glass.

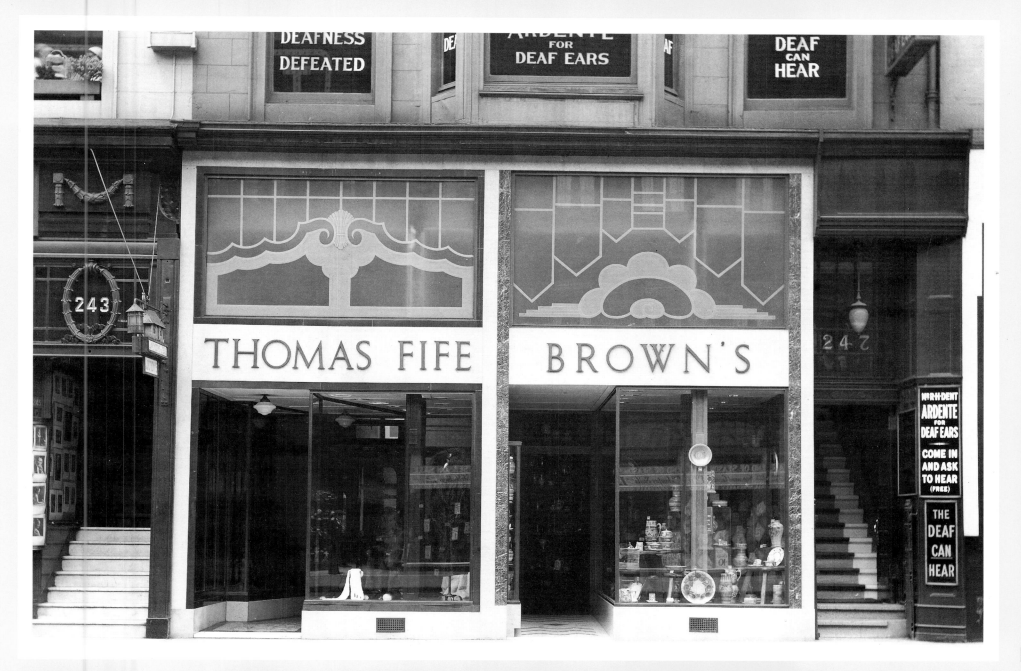

These adjoining shops in Sauchiehall Street, photographed in 1934, display elegant Art Deco transom glass.

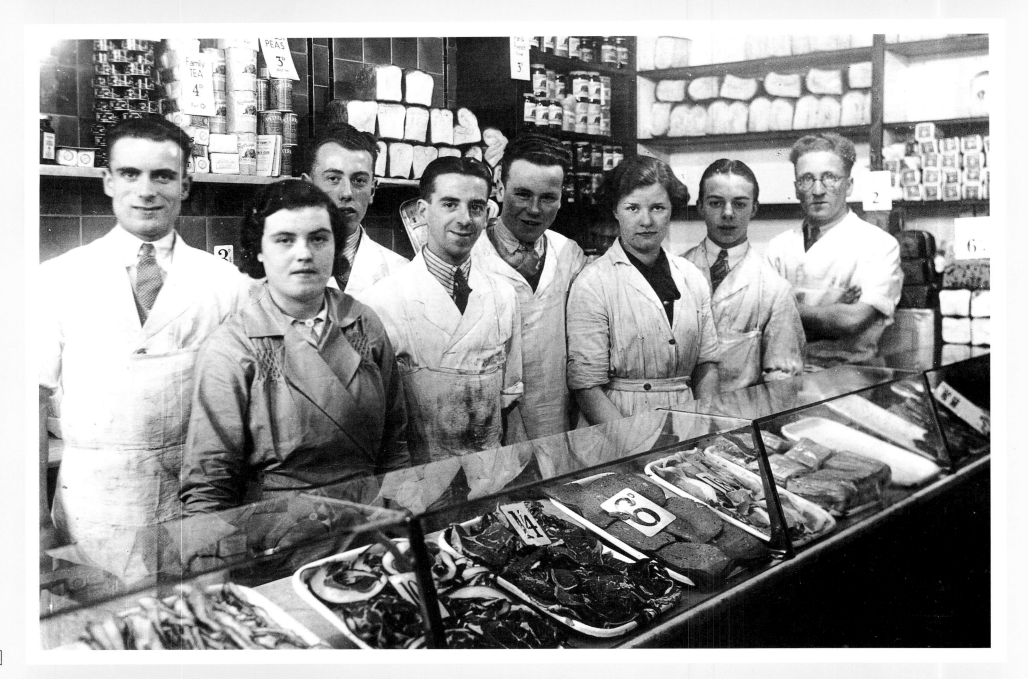

Staff in Lindsay's grocery shop, 61 Parliamentary Road, 1934.

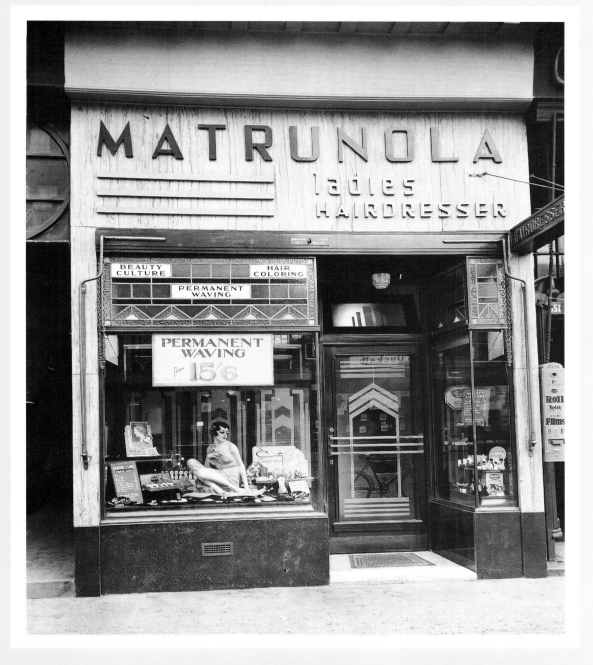

Hairdresser's salon, 1049 Pollokshaws Road, 1934. In the 1930s, Hollywood set high standards of glamour and it was imperative for women to 'keep young and beautiful'.

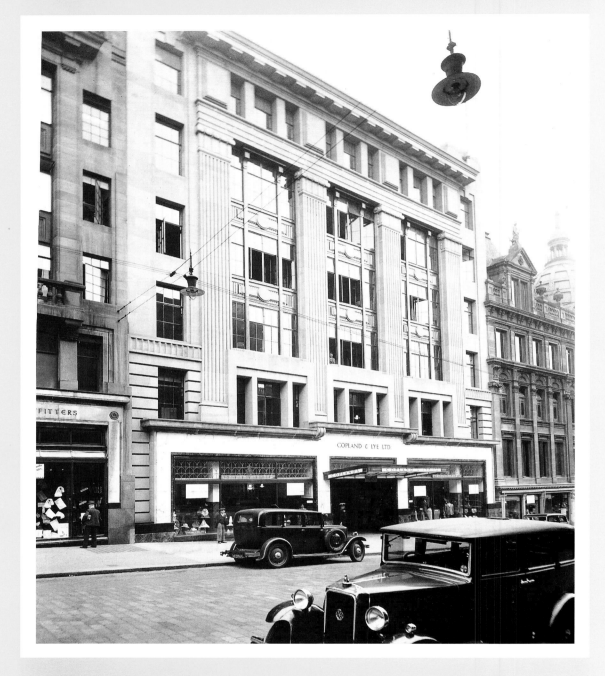

Copland and Lye's new extension in Bath Street was designed by Launcelot Ross in 1934. The metal spandrels between the stone cladding came from the famous Saracen Foundry in Possilpark. The photograph was taken in 1935.

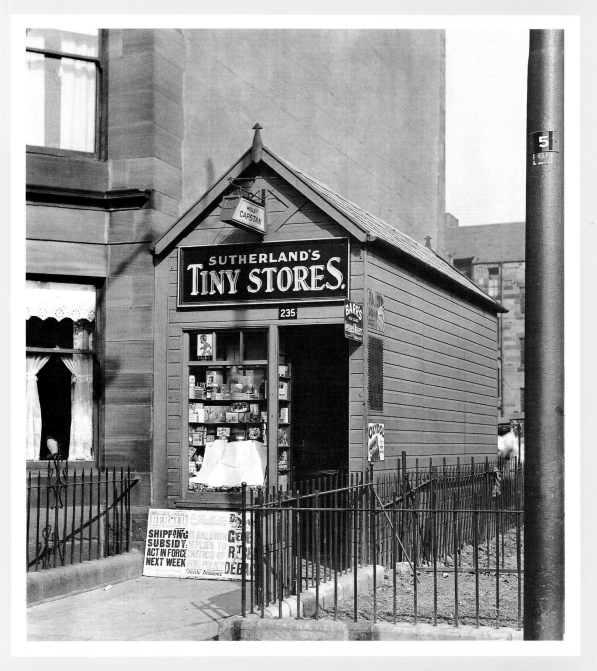

A David in the era of chain store Goliaths, this minimal store, photographed in 1935, was situated at 235 Ledard Road, Langside.

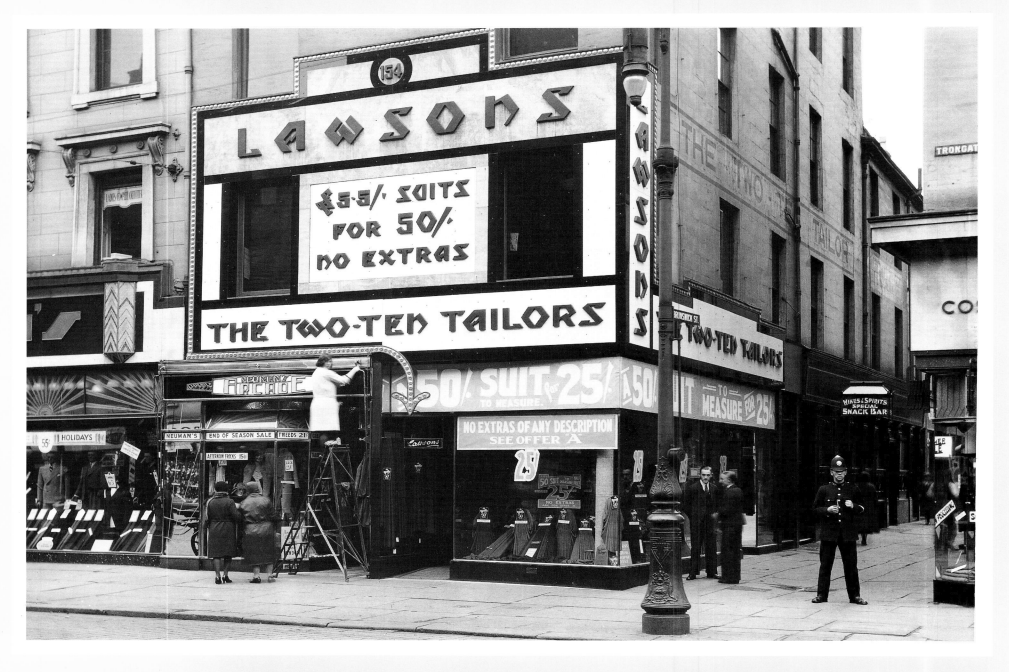

Tailor's shop at 136 Trongate, photographed in 1935, when a gent's suit cost all of £2 10s (£2.50p).

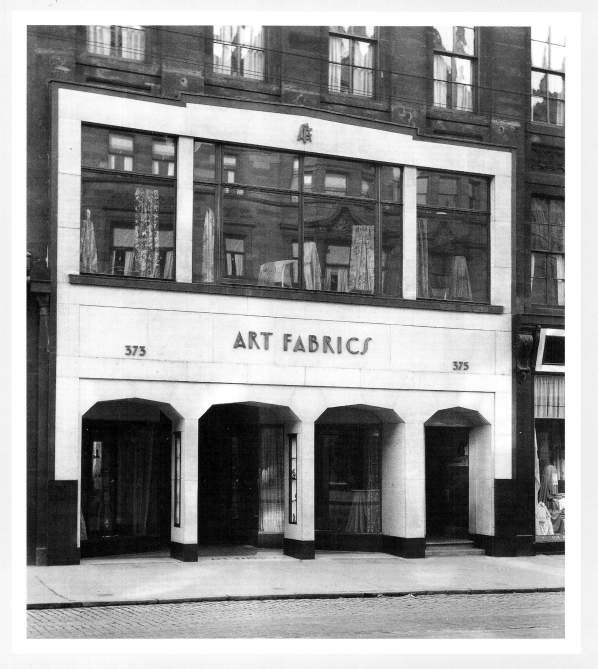

Soft furnishings shop at 373 Sauchiehall Street, photographed in the mid-1930s. One of Glasgow's few remaining Art Deco shop fronts, it was built in 1935 by A. McEwan & Co. to the design of the enterprising London shopfitters Pollard's.

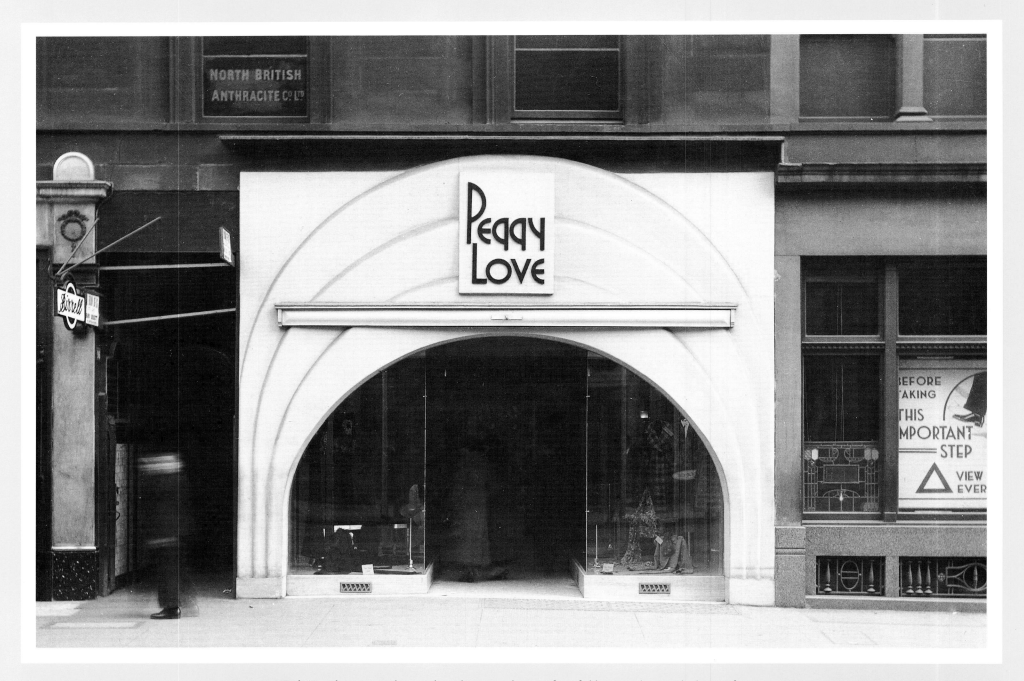

With its striking Art Moderne styling, this gown shop at 96 Renfield Street, photographed in 1936, would not have looked out of place in Sunset Boulevard.

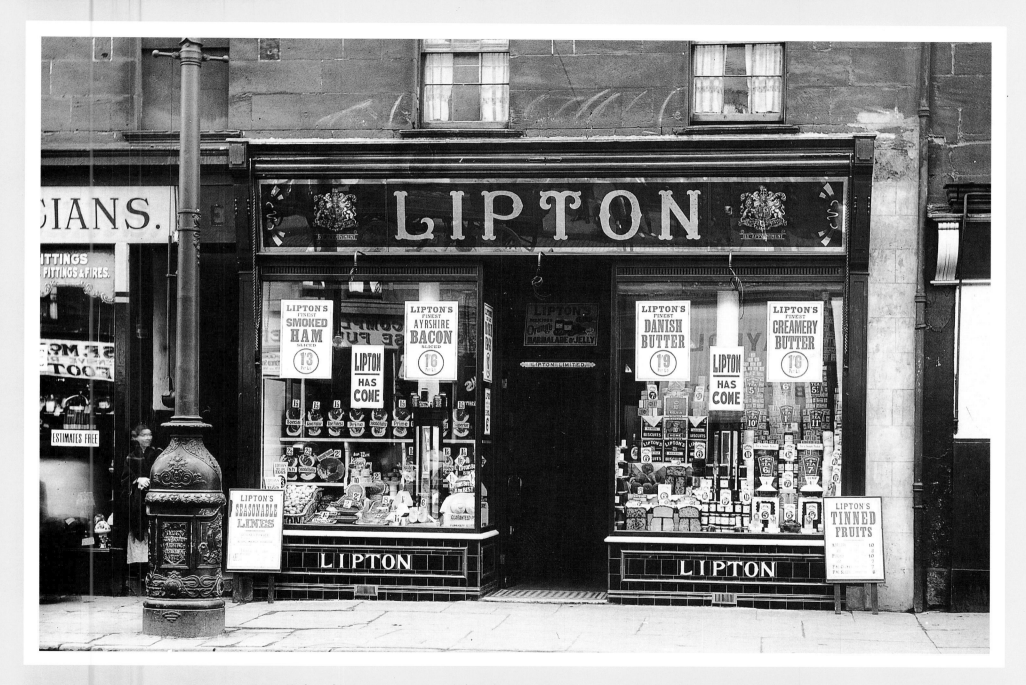

Traditional Lipton's grocery store at 504 Dumbarton Road, photographed in 1936. Chain stores such as Lipton's favoured readily identifiable house-styles.

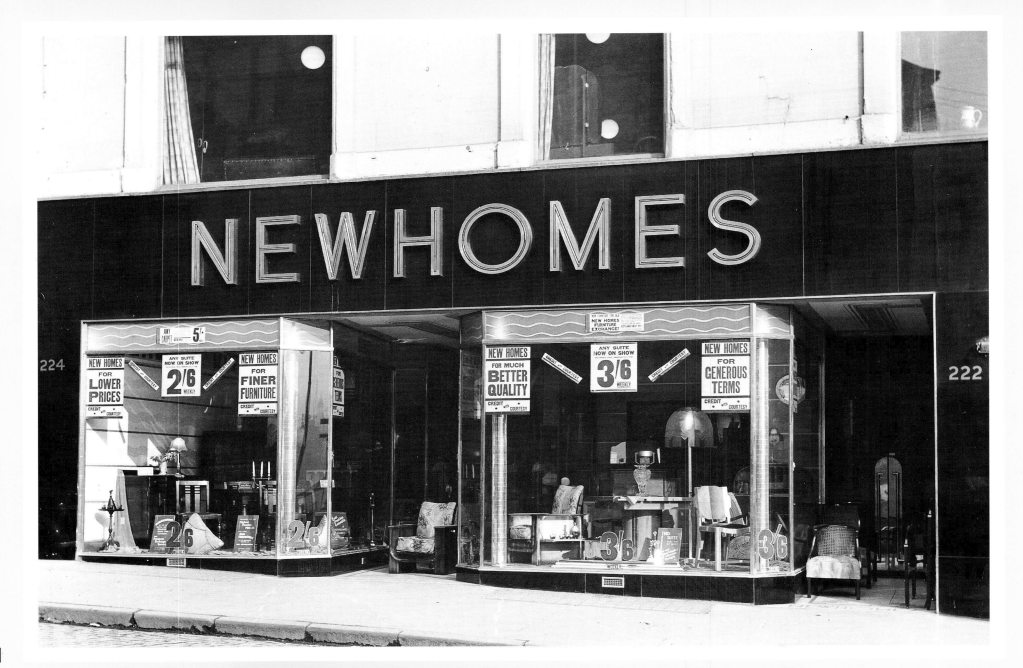

Home furnishings shop at 222-224 Buchanan Street, 1937. In the 1930s, a five-apartment bungalow could be purchased for £850, or 29s weekly, then furnished on 'the instalment plan', familiarly known as 'the never-never'.

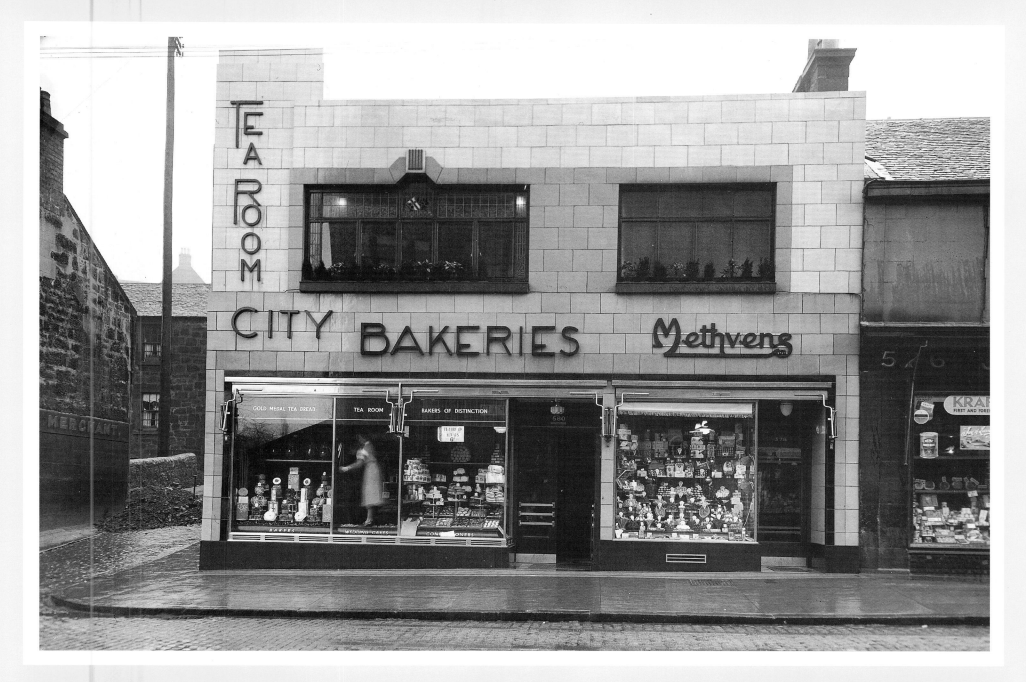

These inviting premises at 578-580 Springburn Road, designed by W. J. B. Wright in 1937, are rendered in fashionable cream, black and grey faience. The photograph was taken in 1939.

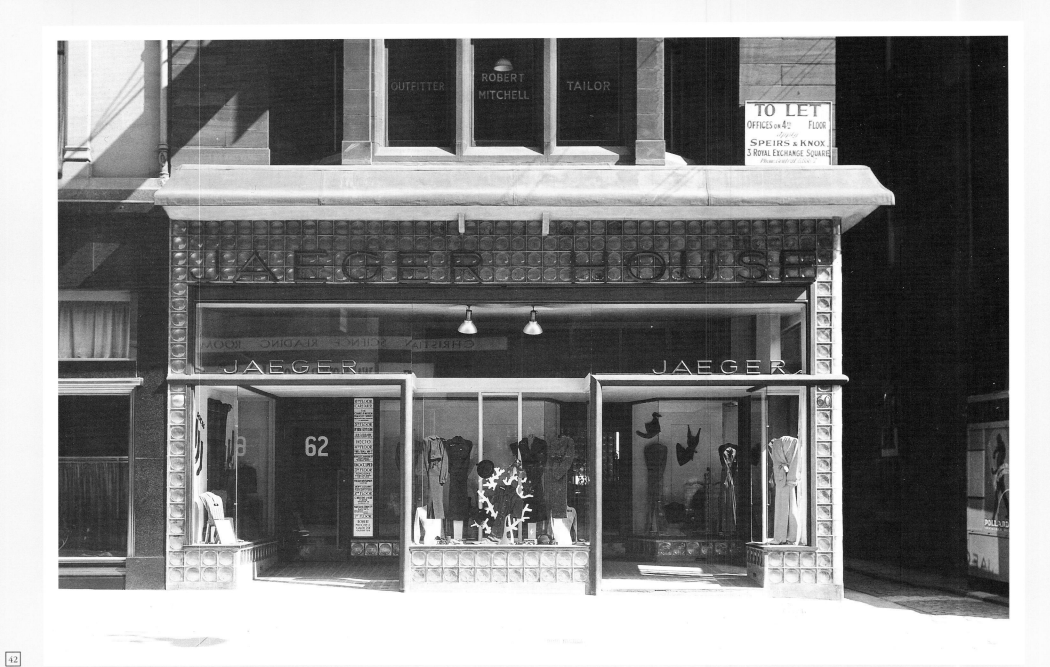

The Jaeger House, 62 Buchanan Street, photographed in 1938. The shop was designed in 1937 by the London-based Modernist John Duncan Miller.

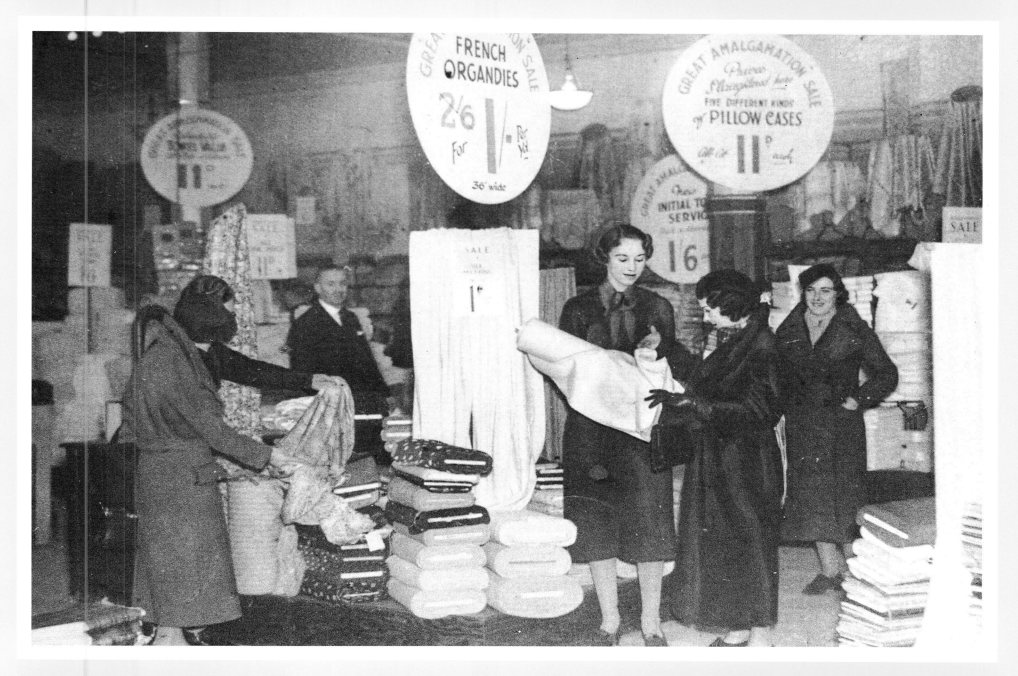

Sale at Arnotts, Argyle Street, February 1938.

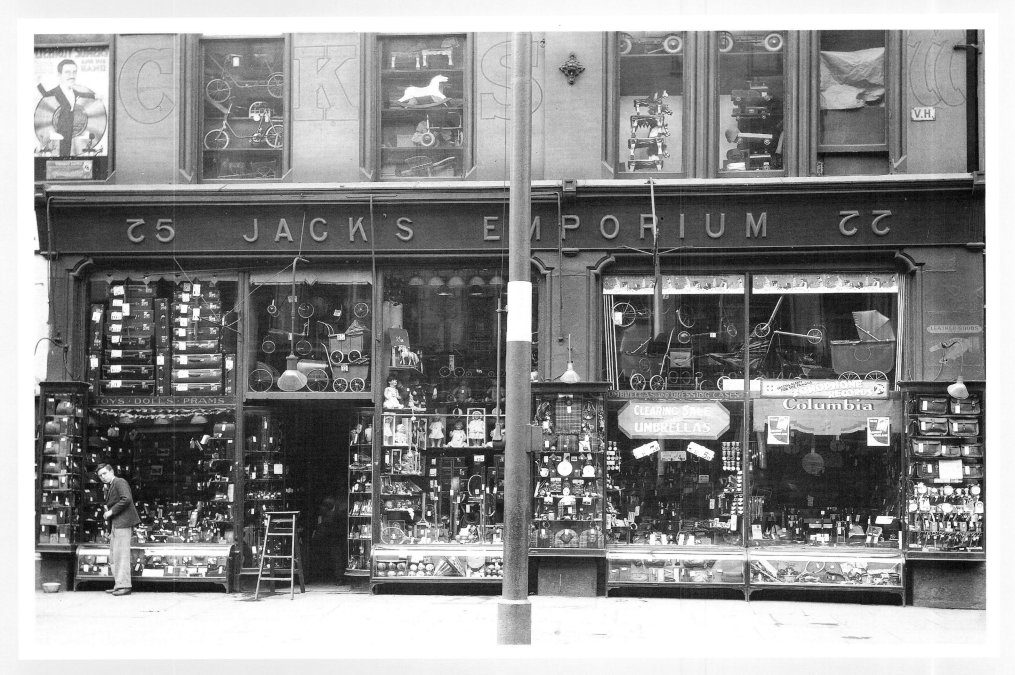

Jack's Emporium, 75 Trongate, 1938. Jack Kay, known as 'Mr. Jack the doll doctor', ran Glasgow's Doll's Hospital.

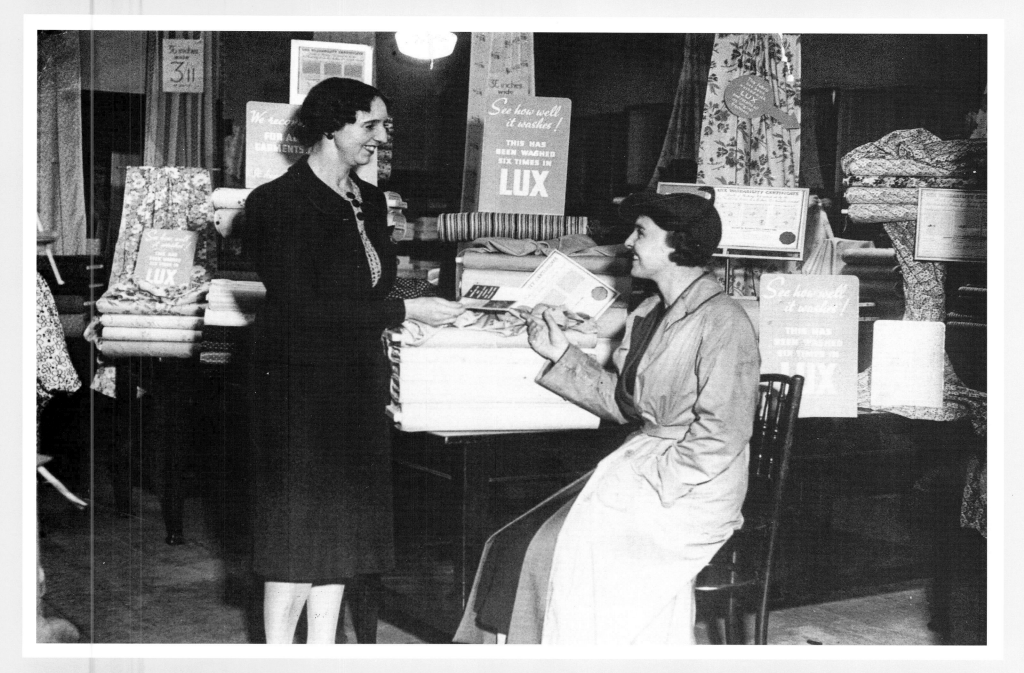

Free advice from the Lux 'washability consultant' in Pettigrew and Stephens' department store, 1938.

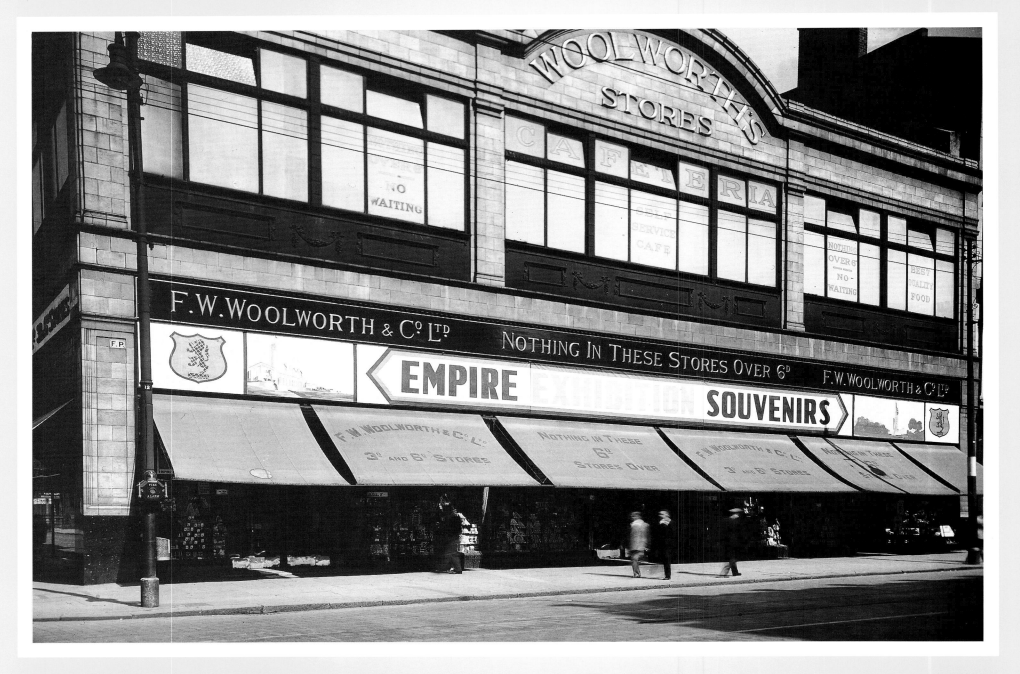

Woolworth's Argyle Street store, photographed in the Empire Exhibition year of 1938.

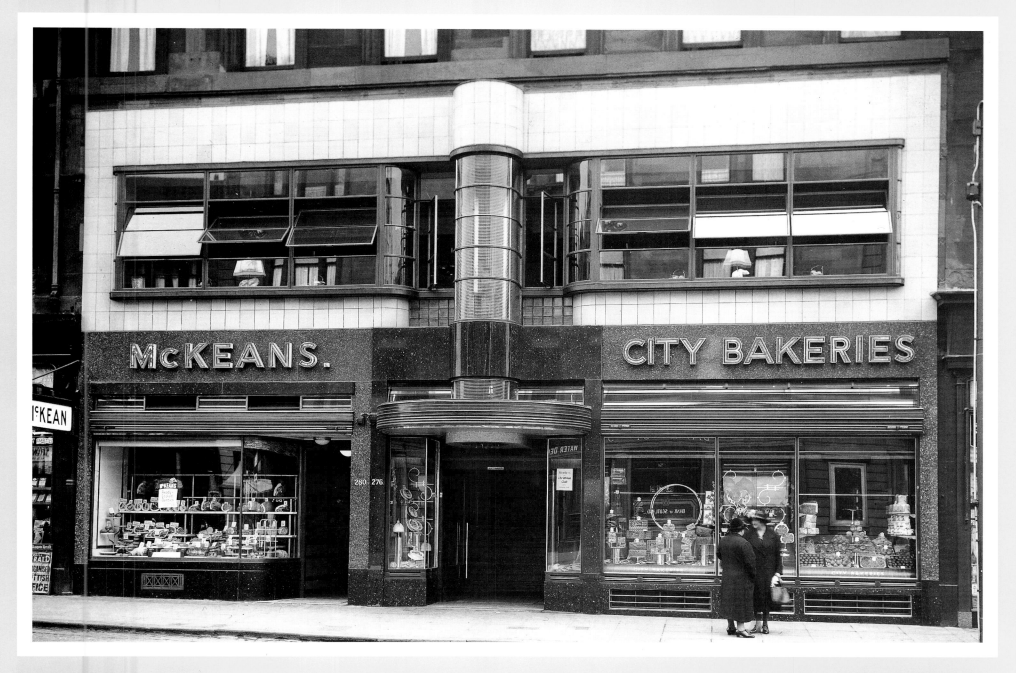

Photographed in 1939, these shop premises at 276-280 St. George's Road reflect the streamlined Art Moderne of the previous year's Empire Exhibition, which brought 13½ million visitors to Bellahouston Park. 'The Grenville House' restaurant occupied the upper storey.

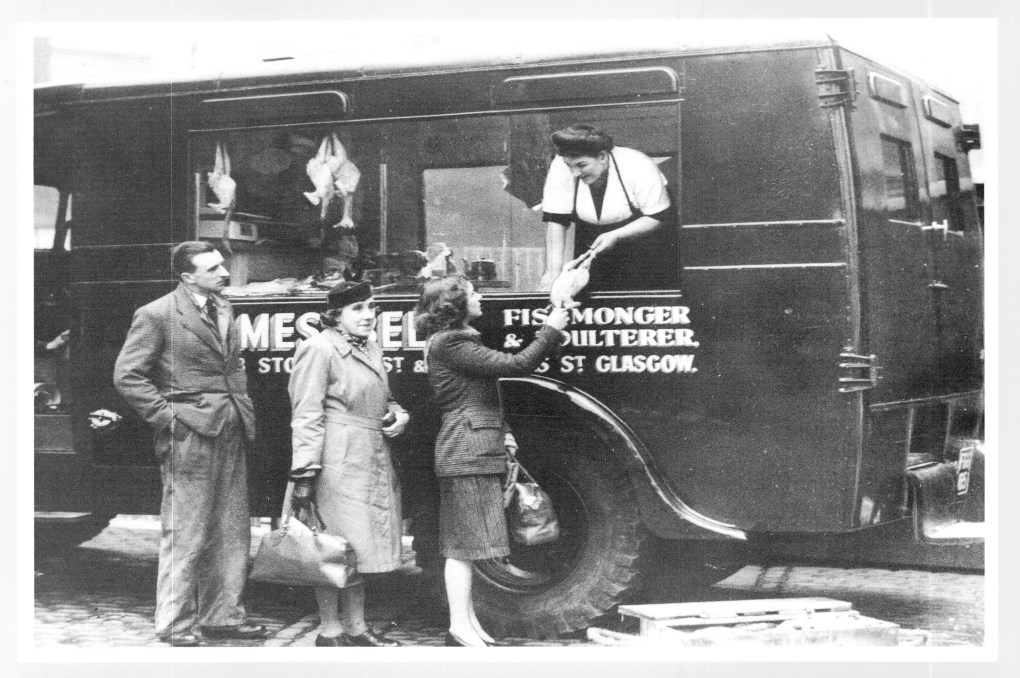

Mobile fish shop in Dundas Street (formerly an RAF ambulance), 1948. Shops on wheels came into their own in the early 1950s, serving the new Corporation housing schemes, which were initially devoid of permanent shops.

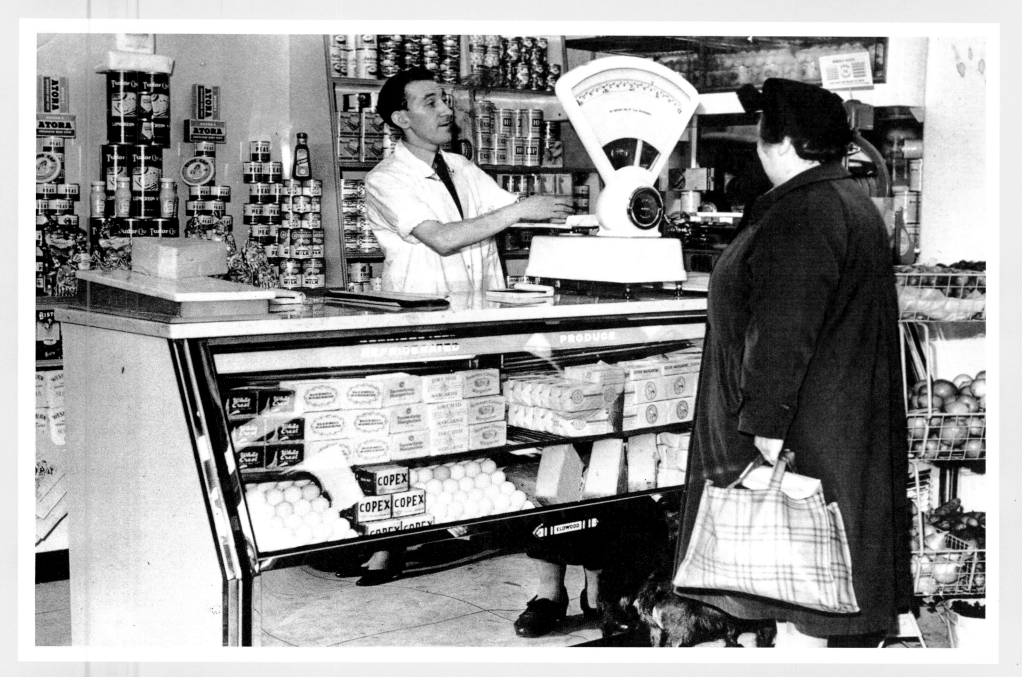

Traditional counter service in the St. George Co-op dairy, 298 St. George's Road, 1955. The 1950s would see the introduction of American-style 'self-service' in many shops.